BEING MAD
A BOOK ABOUT ANGER

Written by
Molly Wigand

Illustrated by
Anne FitzGerald

ABBEY PRESS Publications
1 Hill Drive
St. Meinrad, IN 47577

Text © 2012 Molly Wigand
Illustrations © 2012 St. Meinrad Archabbey
Published by Abbey Press Publications
1 Hill Drive
St. Meinrad, Indiana 47577

Library of Congress Catalog Number
2012905290

ISBN 978-0-87029-502-7

Printed in the United States of America.

A Message from the Author
to Parents and Caring Adults

Children's anger can be upsetting and unsettling to the grown-ups in their worlds. We've all dealt with tantrums and pouting at the least convenient times. If only we could flip a switch on that anger and restore calm to our homes and classrooms.

Of course, there is no such on-and-off switch. The best we can do as caring adults is to help children learn to manage their anger in a way that helps them grow and helps maintain calm environments in which we all can get along.

The world at large isn't helping much, depicting anger in very unhealthy and often violent ways. We need to be vigilant all day, every day, as we monitor our kids' game playing, television watching, and movie going, to make sure they're getting the "right" messages.

On the other hand, schools, churches, and other institutions place high value on our children being compliant and agreeable. But some of these settings can become oppressive, especially when overwhelmed adults demand that kids just sit still and "get with the program." A student's anger can disrupt plans and can land a child in the principal's office.

Our society is confused about anger, to say the least. As spiritually driven adults, we know that God made us capable of all sorts of feelings. But, where anger is concerned, we tend to feel a little less accepting and patient, especially when it comes to parenting a headstrong child.

By helping our children accept and express their anger, this complicated emotion becomes less of a beast. We can become better listeners and teachers, enabling our children to become better equipped to deal with anger when it inevitably pops up in their lives.

—Molly Wigand

All about you!

You are a one-of-a-kind kid. God made you that way, and He loves every part of you. You have your own special face. You have your own special body. And you have your own special feelings. One of those feelings is anger.

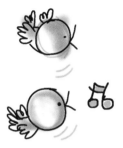

What happens when you're angry?

Anger can be scary. Your heart beats faster. Your face may turn red. You may get all sweaty, or shaky, or even dizzy. Your stomach might hurt. Being angry is a normal part of life. But it's not fun to feel that way.

Why do we get angry?

Your anger lets you know when something is bothering you.

Has anyone ever taken your toy or borrowed your bike without asking? Maybe anger helped you stick up for yourself.

Sometimes your mom gets angry if you don't do your chores. That's normal, too.

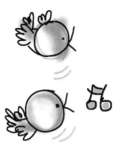

Just keep trying!

It's okay to be angry. Everybody gets angry.

Learning to deal with anger makes you a happier person. It's like learning to read or ride a bike.

Keep practicing and pretty soon you'll be super good at it.

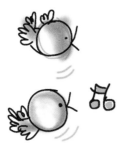

Easy as 1, 2, 3!

Try these three steps to help the angry feelings go away:

1. Count down backwards from 10 to 1.
2. Figure out why you're angry.
3. Tell someone how you feel.

Count down to calm!

Let's practice being angry.

Pretend it's Saturday. Your mom wants you to do your chores. She won't let you play outside. Your friends are all playing, and you are feeling mad.

Take a deep breath in and out.
Then count backwards from 10.

Think about it!

Why are you mad?

Say these words to yourself: "I really want to play outside. I don't like doing chores. Saturdays are for fun! I am very angry! This isn't fair!"

Are you starting to feel better?

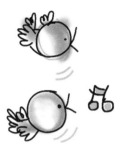

Talk about it!

Now it's time to share your feelings.

Holding in angry feelings makes them bigger. It can even make you sick.

Here's a good way to share your angry feelings. Say this: "Mom, I feel angry when you make me do chores on Saturday."

Take time to listen.

You've told your mom that you are angry and why. Now she understands how you feel. Listen to what she has to say. You can work this out together.

Practice using this special sentence. Use it with friends, family, and teachers.

I feel angry when you _____.

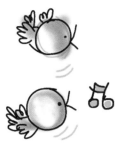

Too mad to talk it out?

What if you're too angry to use your new skills? What if you want to yell or hit or call names?

Hitting or yelling can make your anger worse. You might hurt someone's feelings. You might make your family angry. And you might lose a friend.

Work off some angry energy!

Doing exercise can help with anger.

Find a place away from people. Run or march in place. Do some jumping jacks. Throw a football. Kick a ball. Play some music and dance.

Your body can help you get through your anger.

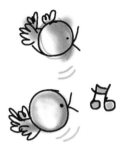

Say a little prayer.

Remember that God knows how you feel.

A simple prayer can really help. You might say, "Help me calm down." Or ask, "Why am I so angry?"

God's love can help melt away your anger.

Nobody's perfect.

Sometimes exercise, prayer, and talking don't seem to work at all. You may hit someone or use mean words to put them down. That's called "unhealthy anger."

When you use unhealthy anger, say you're sorry. Ask the other person to forgive you.

Just do your best.

Most days are happy and fun, but we're all different people, and we don't always get along. God loves you and understands all your feelings, even the angry ones.

Remember the 1, 2, 3 trick?
1. Count down backwards from 10 to 1.
2. Figure out why you're angry.
3. Tell someone how you feel.

With a little practice, learning how to not be angry is as easy as 1, 2, 3.

Molly Wigand is a writer and editor who lives in Lenexa, Kansas. She and her husband, Steve Jackson, have three sons. She is the author of a number of children's books and has taught creative writing to children and adults. She is a frequent contributor to Abbey Press Publications and is the author of the Elf-Help Book for Kids *Help Is Here for Facing Fear*.

Anne FitzGerald is an internationally known artist and has written and illustrated over 200 children's books. She is creator of "Dear God Kids" and many other children's books and products. Anne works from her studio/gallery in Limerick, Ireland, and teaches art in Liberty Christian School there.

For other books in this series go to:
www.abbeypresspublications.com
and click on "JUST FOR ME BOOKS" in the side bar.